HOW TO
CHANGE YOUR HABITS
AND
TRANSFORM YOUR LIFE

A GUIDE TO BUILDING POSITIVE, DAILY ROUTINES TO
HELP MANIFEST THE LIFE YOU'VE ALWAYS WANTED

NICOLE LOCKHART

SPECIAL BONUS!
Want this Bonus Book free?

Get **FREE**, unlimited access to it and all of my new books by joining the Fan Base!

SCAN WITH YOUR CAMERA TO JOIN!

TABLE OF CONTENTS

INTRODUCTION

Are you ready to make some changes to your Daily Habits to attract the life you've always wanted?

We all have a limited amount of energy to use up each day, will you choose to use it on healthy productive habits or will you let bad habits rob you of your best future and of reaching your dreams and goals?

After writing my last book, "365 Days of Positive Affirmations" all geared towards "change" in your life so that you can reach your big goals quickly and efficiently, I realized there was something else holding us back from using daily affirmations and reaching our goals quickly! Bad habits are keeping us stuck and the lack of new good habits are keeping us from speedily and consistently reaching our big goals!

The secrets of success are hiding behind our bad habits and routines. Bad habits trick us into thinking they're making us happy when they're really keeping us from achieving what we want most in life. Millions of people suffer from habits that are holding them back from their best lives. Obvious bad habits include drinking alcohol, smoking cigarettes, poor diet, not getting enough exercise or too much stress, but there are many others as well that are less obvious. Some are hard to identify and we don't even know how much they hold us back.

I am going to discuss the bad habits holding us back and some good habits to replace them. These are prominent areas that many people want to change in some way:

- Wealth
- Health and Healing
- Happiness
- Love and/or Meaningful Human Connection
- Self-Confidence and Self-Esteem
- Extreme Habits

If you have other areas in your life that you want to work on, no problem! These are just the top examples that I have found most people struggle with. You can use my methods and templates to change any habits and help you get to your goals faster!

I think most of us can agree that we all want more of these things in our life. But how to get there. It all starts with goals and plans. Dream big and make a list of your goals and dreams. Once you have your mind set on your destination, we will fill in the pieces to get you there. Imagine you are traveling across the country. You've never been there before but you have a destination. You have to take each mile at a time and focus on it to arrive safely. You need to check your directions along the way. The scenery will change and almost everything will change as you travel closer to your destination. You may have to alter your path if you go off course. And you will need to take time to rest along the way.

Bad habits are like getting a flat tire, not only once a day, but multiple times! Every time you get a flat tire you have to stop, probably spend some money, change the tire, and off you go again. Because habits are stored in the automatic part of your brain, you don't even question why you're doing them. Using the traveling analogy, you could question: maybe your tires aren't very good, maybe you're driving too fast or maybe you're on the wrong road altogether.

The same is true if your goal is a certain amount of money or a personal health target. Bad habits slow us down and use up our resources. PLEASE download my free book "Creating A Vision Board". This is will help you set some big goals, replace some of your bad habits with some productive ones, and begin to transform your life!

The Universe works like a magnet. Once you do the right work to yourself by changing your habits to be positive and productive, instead of negative and destructive, the things, people, relationships and everything else you've always wanted will come to you.

Daily habits can hold you back from the path to your dreams. So let's make sure you develop some good ones. You will learn to identify and get rid of old bad habits and replace them with good habits that benefit your life and your long-term goals.

CHAPTER 1:

WHY CHANGE YOUR HABITS?

What are habits, and how do they impact our life?

Change your habits and transform your life. It's no coincidence that the word "habit" is derived from the Latin word "habitare" which means "to dwell." Habits are something we do all day long, even when we're not aware of it. They offer a glimpse into our true selves: what we value, what scares us, and how much control we feel over our lives.

If you want to just add some positive, healthy habits into your life, then it is easy. Incorporate them into your daily routine and they will soon become automatic. If you are wanting to get rid of a bad habit, then it is a little more complicated and requires some perseverance, determination, willpower and a good plan!

We can cultivate positive habits to help us be happier and healthier or destructive ones to make us feel helpless.

When changing a bad habit, there are three things to keep in mind:

- awareness (knowing which behaviors you want to change)
- motivation (having a reason why this new behavioral routine will benefit you in some way)
- and accountability (keeping track of your progress)

Daily habits are like tiny building blocks. Each day, are you building a healthy body? A good financial plan for your future? Every little thing you do is either building the thing you want or building something else. If you choose a donut for a snack instead of a piece of fruit, you are building an unhealthy body, not a healthy one. If you spend your money frivolously on fancy dining and entertaining nights out you are building a less than robust financial future for yourself, instead of a solid and profitable one.

How do Habits form?

Habits become your routine. The more you do them, the harder they are to break. You may already have some good habits, like keeping your kitchen clean or eating a good diet. But you may want to identify some habits that are hindering your ultimate plan to reaching your goals and living your best life.

Habits can start off as part of a conscious goal but quickly become automatic and subconscious. The American Journal of Psychology defines a "habit" as a more or less fixed way of thinking, willing, or feeling acquired through previous repetition of a mental experience. New behaviors can become automatic through the process of habit formation. The behavioral patterns of habit become imprinted in neural pathways, making old habits hard to break and new ones hard to form, but by using repetition, new habits can form and replace bad ones.

Habit formation has three main parts, the context cue, the behavioral repetition and the reward. This is known as the habit loop. We will talk about breaking or changing the habit loop in the coming Chapters. Recognizing and eliminating bad habits as soon as possible is advised because as we age the habits become more ingrained in our neural pathways. It doesn't mean that you will be stuck with a bad habit forever, it just requires more effort to change or replace a long-standing bad habit.

We all have a certain amount of energy to expend each day. Will you choose to use it on habits that leave you feeling unhealthy, broke, alone and hopeless? Or will you make an effort to only expend your daily energy on habits that promote a healthy body, solid financial future and a life full of meaningful relationships?

Qualities of Good Habits

*They benefit you. Are your daily habits contributing to a healthy body and mind? Are you making choices that your future self will be proud of? Are you saving money for your future? Do you have a balance of rest and work?

*They benefit others. Anytime win-win is at work, you know you have a good habit. Good habits are often synergistic, they are good for you and good for others.

*They are enjoyable. When you start a new habit it might not feel that enjoyable right away, there might be a period of mourning for your old destructive habit. But in time your positive habit will be enjoyable. For example, walking or running every day. At first, you might be missing your couch, but in time you will get used to the endorphins and good feelings that come from walking or running regularly.

*They are productive. They produce a healthy body, mind or benefit your life in some way. They are often forward-looking and contribute to your big picture and long-term goals.

*They involve action. They involve "doing" something. I don't mean watching TV or social media, I mean creating something, caring for yourself or someone else, and thinking of your future.

*They promote your health. Good health habits might seem obvious, but you might need some help identifying which of your health habits are actually good habits. You will be able to use the templates in Chapter 10 to help you become aware of some of your health habits.

*They have a long-term goal attached to themselves. Many good habits will pay off in the future. Exercising daily, eating healthily, saving money, all will benefit your future self.

*They are honest and have integrity. Good habits are always honest and true. Not just true for you but true for the Universe. Good habits are universally good and are based on strong moral principles.

*They encourage self-discipline. By choosing to focus on creating good habits, it will help you when temptation arises. Self-discipline is a muscle, the more you use it, the stronger it gets.

*They are constructive with your big picture goals. Good habits will help you build the future that you've always wanted. You may not see results right away, but rest assured, your good habits are building blocks for your best future self and life.

Qualities of Bad habits

*They harm you or others. Some habits such as smoking or over-eating are pretty obviously bad for your own body. But there are many other habits that aren't as clear, cut and dried. You might think your habit isn't harming anyone other than yourself, but when you dig a little deeper, you will see that most habits that harm yourself, will also have an effect down the line of harming others. Second-hand smoke is an obvious one and for over-eating, your friends and family might be missing out on a healthy energetic "you".

*They destroy synergy. Bad habits are not synergistic. They are the opposite, they repulse others that would otherwise be good friends or companions away from us, and we end up with others that share our bad habits.

*They are not productive. Over time our bad habits leave us with nothing. Our bodies become unhealthy, our bank accounts become empty and you have nothing to show from all your daily habit energy.

*They cost you your health or your money. Most bad habits will end up costing you your health or your money at some point. It may not seem obvious when you're young and full of youthful energy, but over time, bad habits take a toll.

*They are destructive of your big picture goals. Bad habits will keep you pacified for today but will they create the future you've always dreamt of having? No, they will not. They rob you of your dreams and goals, not right away but long-term you will be left with nothing and only then you will see what bad habits have stolen from you. Let me help you be proactive today so that you can have the future that you've always wanted.

CHAPTER 2:

WHY IS IT SO HARD TO CHANGE YOUR HABITS?

"Old habits die hard." The only way to win against this old quote is perseverance and a good plan. You need to pull out all the stops and use affirmations, visualizations, lists and the templates in Chapter 10 of this book. You need to develop your perseverance and willpower. You will become stronger and stronger as you take it one day at a time.

Awareness is a good place to begin, start thinking about when your bad habits creep in, when does it happen, who are you with, where are you, what is the trigger/cue, does it happen right after something else? Practice mindfulness, simply observe the impulses that relate to your bad habit without judging or reacting, just become aware and write them down.

Changing anything can be hard. Our brains become wired to think something is normal and then when you suddenly change it, your brain is left with a gap. It feels like something is missing. Sometimes we know a habit is bad for us, but our brains will fight as if our existence depended on perpetuating the bad habit. The habit-forming behaviors are linked to the basal-ganglia, also known as the "autopilot" part of our brain. No wonder it is so hard to break them!

Breaking the Habit loop.

The best way to change anything is to REPLACE it with something more powerful and positive. In the next chapter, you will learn the 3 parts of habits. The context cue, the behavioral routine and the reward and will talk about replacing one or all of the parts to break the bad habit cycle. This is why "just say no" doesn't work. The right answer is "just say yes" to a more positive routine that fulfills the reward of your cue or trigger.

New routines could include:
Choosing gum to replace a cigarette, when you get the smoking urge
Choosing a piece of fruit to replace a sugary snack, when you have a sugar craving

Going for a walk to replace lying on the couch, when you get home from work

Another reason why it is so hard is because most of us don't do it right. A big thing many of us get wrong is positive vs. negative phrasing.

Many studies have shown that positive phrasing is more powerful than negative phrasing. Remember this when you choose the habits that you want to start changing. Be patient with yourself and always think of the positive thing you are gaining instead of the negative thing you are trying to get rid of or stop doing.

How to phrase your goals in a positive way:
A classic example is the notoriously bad habit of smoking. Instead of making your goal "to quit smoking" make it "to have pink, clean, healthy lungs".

Instead of making your goal "to be less lazy" make your goal "to find exercise that I enjoy".

Instead of making your goal "to stop being broke all the time" make your goal "to earn a certain amount of money that will cover all my needs".

By phrasing your goals and routines positively, you are incredibly helping your subconscious to help you reach your goals. Your brain doesn't know what to do with negatives, it gets stuck and just goes in circles. All your brain hears is "smoke, lazy, broke". Your mind gets confused as to why you would want to focus on those things. But with positive goals, your mind hears "clean, healthy, exercise, money" and it's full speed ahead to achieve success!

Now that you are committed to making some habit changes to help you reach your big picture goals, help your brain even more by making some colorful posters that envision your new habit. Write down some of your favorite positive affirmations to get you there faster and more efficiently.

What causes Bad Habits?

Stress, boredom and loneliness are the main causes of bad habits. The "habit loop" starts often when we are young and becomes stronger and stronger as the years go by. The basal ganglia part of our brain is not only linked to habits but also to the development of emotions, memories and pattern recognition. This is helpful for productive automatic routines like brushing your teeth or parallel parking, but not for destructive habits.

Once a specific behavior becomes automatic, our free will and decision-making part of our brain, the prefrontal cortex, thinks that these automatic behaviors are taking care of themselves and turns off from recognizing them so it can focus on other day-to-day decisions. Your prefrontal cortex doesn't distinguish between good automatic behaviors and bad automatic behaviors.

Often bad habits can start because we are trying to fill a void. Maybe you didn't get support or love from your parents and started smoking or eating too much junk food. Many bad habits stem back decades and you will have to go back in time to discover the motivations for starting. Once you've done that, you can try to find some replacement habits that fulfill the need that was never fulfilled to start with. Use Template 3 in Chapter 10.

Conditions that require professional help.

This book is not a replacement for medical or professional help. These are some conditions that you will likely need additional support to overcome.

Compulsions and Obsessive-Compulsive Disorder (OCD). Compulsive acts can start when someone tries to fight their anxious or intrusive thoughts with a purposeful, deliberate action (can be physical or mental). The behavior soon becomes automatic and can be overwhelming and consuming.

Addictions and substance use. These conditions can start off recreationally and quickly lead to a more serious dependency-like condition. You will likely need professional help to stop these cases.

Smoking. Some people can stop smoking on their own, but many require multiple layers of support including counseling or medication from a medical doctor. Smoking can start as a bad habit but soon becomes a physical and psychological dependency situation.

Eating disorders. Any type of eating disorder should not be taken lightly. They can stem from bad eating habits and soon evolve into sometimes life-threatening conditions. Seek professional help if you have any type of eating disorder.

We will talk more about these conditions in Chapter 9.

The False feeling of Deserving.

Have you ever felt like you deserved that extra drink because you worked hard, or felt like you deserved a piece of cake because you exercised last week? I have been studying deserving for a while and it is easy to see the downside of it just by looking at some specific celebrities. I won't mention any names but numerous big stars have ended up addicted, cheating on their spouses, wasting their money, or just wasting their lives in general. When they finally reach rock bottom and are able to talk about what has happened, time and time again, they say "I felt like I deserved it". Meaning they deserved the mistresses, drugs and phony good times because of who they are and their acclaimed celebrity success. Feeling like you deserve can also lead to developing bad habits and in extreme cases, addiction, substance use and other life-wasting conditions. Try to change your mindset about deserving.

Grace.

Instead of "deserving" think "grace". Grace might sound religious to you, but it didn't start out that way, it is a very old word with Latin origin. The Merriam-Webster dictionary says grace is "unmerited divine assistance given to humans for their regeneration or sanctification", or "a state of sanctification enjoyed through divine assistance".

Grace is letting the Universe fit you in where you belong. By trusting that the Universe will put you in the way of many good things will in fact, ensure that the benefits/rewards of your hard work are positive, healthy and satisfy your life goals. When we make up our own benefits/rewards because we think we deserve them, time and time again we choose wrong.

I am not saying don't strive for your new car, house, or life partner. That is exactly what I want you to have. Set big goals and find your way to get them. But HOW you get them is important. If you feel "deserving" you might be tempted to cut corners or choose the quick-fix way to your goal, or completely forget your goal because of some short-term good times. Keep your eye on the prize. Set your big goals and change your habits to get there safely and as soon as possible without wasting time. Have faith that the Universe is helping you.

It is no coincidence that "grace" and "gratitude" start with the same three letters. Both of these words come from Latin origin meaning "pleasing, thankful". Developing a grateful attitude will ensure you are living a graceful life, attuned to the Universe, where all your dreams and goals can become reality. You can use my book "One Year of Gratitude Journaling" to get started.

Make your own luck.

People that are attuned to the universe and living in a graceful state are sometimes seen as being "lucky". Good things just seem to happen regularly for people living like this. The good news is, you can make your own luck! When you dig deep and find out what really makes you happy and which long-term goals you want to achieve, get yourself on the right path, and practice gratitude, everything will fall into place. Things will just start working out for you, and you will have good fortune not just from chance, but because you put yourself in the path of all the good things that you want in life.

When you are doing all the right steps to manifesting your goals, you are walking in grace, the Universe will give you what you need, when you need it. Trust that by doing the right work upfront, and being patient, the Universe will pull your goals to you like a magnet, all in perfect and due time. And when you get them the right way, they will stick to you magnetically.

CHAPTER 3:

THE BEST WAYS TO CHANGE YOUR HABITS.

What is preventing you from getting to your Big Goals? Do you need more money? A healthier body? More time to meet people? Try to find the negative thing that you do regularly that is hindering your progress to your goals. Read through the "bad habits" listed for each of the following Chapters. There will be some things that you are doing daily you might not even realize are keeping you from reaching your goals.

Chapter 10 of this book, has some templates to help you identify the habits that you want to change and help you keep on track when developing new ones. Make written or visual plans for changing your habits, make as many as you need and put them in places where you will see them regularly.

Break the Cycle

Every habit is based on a cycle: the context cue, the behavioral repetition (routine) and the reward/benefit. Or the 3 R's reminder (cue), routine, reward. This is known as the habit loop.

First, become aware of your bad habit:

1. Identify the cue for your bad habit (ex. break time at work, needing a sugar rush for energy when you are hungry and craving a donut)
2. Identify the routine (eating the donut at break time)
3. Identify the reward (energy and a full stomach)

Once you have identified these three characteristics of your bad habit, you can try to eliminate the cue if possible. In this case, the cue can't be eliminated so the next option is changing a bad habit routine. Replace the middle step (the routine) with something positive that satisfies the reward. Make a list of possible choices. Once you feel the cue/trigger coming on, check out your list and have an arsenal of healthy choices waiting in the wings. A banana is high in healthy sugar, potatoes and starchy fruits and vegetables can also satisfy a sugar craving in a healthy way.

Here are some different approaches to eliminating bad habits and forming new ones. They can be used together or separately, some may work for some habits and some may not. As you learn more about yourself, your habits and your motivations for eliminating habits and forming new ones, you will get clearer on how to use these strategies. Be sure to use the Templates in Chapter 10 to help you make a plan to break some old habits and form some new ones.

Remove the Cue/Urge/Trigger.

This is also known as *withdrawal of reinforcers* – identifying and removing factors that trigger and reinforce the habit. If you have a drinking problem, don't go to the bar, if you have a sweet tooth don't bring sugary snacks into the house and leave them lying around. This will make it easier for you as you form new habits to replace old ones. Change or alter your environment and avoid, avoid, avoid. Write out some one-liners if your habit has a social basis so that you are ready when you're asked to put yourself in an environment that contributes to or triggers your bad habit.

If you can't eliminate the Cue, replace the Routine and add in more Rewards.

Some cues we can't eliminate, for example getting home after work, can trigger us to feel like lying on the couch. Although we can't eliminate this cue, we can replace the routine by going for a walk instead of lying on the couch.

Here is an example of how to make a positive habit-changing statement to hang on your wall where you feel your cue, in this case, the entrance hall.

1. Identify the cue, when and where does it happen?
2. Identify the routine you want to change and phrase it in a positive way about what you are gaining, instead of what you are giving up. Write it down.

   Example: "I want to get more exercise" (Instead of "I feel tired and want to lie on the couch")

3. Add in some benefits/rewards to your statement.

   Example: "I want to get more exercise so that I have more energy and to be healthy."

   Example: "When I get home from work, I feel like lying on the couch."

Replace it with: "When I get home from work I feel like going for a 10-minute power walk so I will have energy and feel healthy."

4. Now that you know what to do, put your plan (using Template 5) up on the wall near your front door. For this habit, the cue happens around 4:30 pm each day, so be ready. When your cue comes up at 4:30 it's time for the Big Guns, keep your templates, vision board and positive affirmations by your front door, before you even take your shoes off, go for your walk!

In addition to the specific habits listed for each topic in the following Chapters, the best things you can do daily once you have created some big goals, is to create a vision board for your goals and use daily positive affirmations to re-program your brain.

Visualization. Studies have shown that there is a super-power to visualization. You've probably heard about the basketball experiment by Australian psychologist Alan Richardson. He divided players into three groups and did an experiment for 20 days. The first group practiced free throws every day. The second group did free throws on the first and 20th day as did the third group. But the third group visualized their free throws for 20 minutes a day for days 2-19. When it came time to test the progress on the 20th day, the first group had improved by 24%, the second group not at all, and the third group improved 23%! Nearly the same as the actual practicing group. Visualization is powerful for your success, take some time to surround yourself with photos that describe your new habits and lifestyle. Then spend a certain amount of time each day envisioning yourself doing your new habit.

You can also visualize yourself breaking a bad habit and envision yourself reacting differently. This is a good time to practice some deep breathing exercises as you might feel anticipation or nervousness. You can use a fidget toy if you need help staying calm and repeat some of your favorite affirmations as well.

Positive Affirmations are like snow tires in the blizzard of life. Now that you have identified some habits that you want to change, phrased them positively, added in some benefits and are aware of your bad habit cue and routine, I suggest using positive affirmations to make your new habit easier to achieve. Once you are on the path to your goals, affirmations will get you there faster and safely with no chance of going off the track. By repeating some well-thought-out and well-chosen affirmations, your brain will become effectively reprogrammed. It will think the things you are wanting are now normal and the Universe will bring them to you.

What the mind can conceive and believe it can achieve. Your brain is the original super-computer, if you are not where you currently want to be in your life, it's time for some reprogramming. I have listed some of my favorite and most powerful positive affirmations after each chapter. Choose your favorites and write them on a piece of paper but them in your bathroom, kitchen, or car so that you can see them regularly throughout the day. You can also read my book "365 Days of Positive Affirmations" for a daily guide and added ammunition for this journey you are embarking on to create the life that you want. Affirmations are always spoken in the present tense. This way your brain hears the affirmation as if it is already happening. You believe it is happening before it is your reality and the thing you are wanting is magnetically drawn to you.

Doing a 180.

Limiting beliefs keep us stuck. The best way to combat limiting beliefs is with positive affirmations. If you are wanting to get more exercise because you feel overweight or have no energy, tell yourself "I am fit and am full of energy." This is sort of like using positive affirmations but it is an "opposite" affirmation activity. If you think you are not a good cook, tell yourself "I am a good cook." This will make your brain think you really are a good cook and you will start feeling more adventurous and productive in the kitchen.

This might seem a bit odd that you're telling yourself, "I am rich", when you're struggling to pay your bills. Your conscious mind knows that it doesn't reflect your current reality. But your subconscious mind is hard at work and doesn't realize that it is not your current reality. All your powerful subconscious hears is "I am rich", you will start to feel like it is a part of who you are and riches and wealth will soon be drawn to you.

Make a list of the habits that you want to change and tackle them one at a time.

You might not know where to start. You might be wanting a certain lifestyle but not know how to get there. That's ok! Take some time to get to know yourself, your bad habits and your good ones. Use Template 2 in Chapter 10 to identify some bad habits that you may want to change. Tackle them one by one.

Be patient with yourself, allow slip-ups.

We are all human, two steps forward, one step back is reality sometimes. Slip-ups happen. Use a growth mindset, tell yourself *"next time* I will do it differently", "I haven't been able to do it *yet"*, *"but* I'm working hard to reach my goals."

It took a long time to build your habits and it will take some time and dedication to break them.

Self-discipline and good old-fashioned willpower will grow with time and practice, just like a muscle. Template 7 will help you become aware of why you had a slip-up and help you come up with a plan for *next time*.

Join forces with someone that has the same habit or lifestyle goals.

Find a friend, someone that wants to go to the gym with you every day or hang out and watch movies on the weekend to avoid public houses, etc. If your habits are deeper and more dangerous you will need to seek help from a professional. Serious conditions include compulsions, substance use, addiction, or emotional eating.

Reminders.

Set yourself up for success, if you are hooked on social media, invest in some crafts, books, journals and other activities to keep you busy. Place them ahead of time in the places where you scroll for hours on your phone or computer. Put sticky notes with affirmations and reminders in spots where you are triggered to start an unhealthy habit. Or put pieces of fruit waiting for you where you might sit when you crave a sugary snack.

Baby steps. It's not all or nothing.

Eliminating habits and forming new ones is a progression so celebrate the baby steps. If your goal is to stop smoking, keep track of lowering the daily amount of cigarettes that you smoke each day. If you can get down to one, then you can come up with some new ideas to stop completely. If you are working on forming a new habit of eating fruit daily, celebrate each day you remember and do your new habit. Use the Templates in Chapter 10, Template 8 for Bad Habit Daily Progress and Template 10 for Good Habit Daily Progress.

Take a vacation.

If you want to break a bad habit, do it on a holiday. When you are on a holiday, your environment is changed so much that your cues, routines and rewards are all different as well. Everything is out of order, it is a naturally good time to break a habit loop and replace some routines or avoid a cue altogether.

How long does it take to break a habit?

It used to be thought that most habits could be changed in about 21 days but now most experts agree it takes about 10 weeks (about 2-3 months) of repetition and dedication to break a habit. Each habit will be different and depend on how long you've had the habit, the emotional or physical needs of your habit, whether or not you have support and the physical or emotional reward the habit provides.

For Chapters 4-8, I have listed bad habits first and then some good ones that you can use to replace bad habits if you are not already doing them. I've listed the bad habits first because bad habits are the problem! No one ever complains about good habits ruining their life. If you can replace a bad habit with a good one, it's a double gain, losing the bad one and gaining the good one. I know you can do it! Use the templates in Chapter 10, positive affirmations, visualization and all the other ideas contained in this book and don't give up until your new habit wins out!

Positive Affirmations for Change

"Change happens quickly and easily."

"I let go of all that doesn't serve me, to make room for new healthy routines."

"I have everything I need to change my life."

"I am ready for change."

"I am filled with trust that change will happen and bring good into my life."

"I am in control of my life."

"I make changes in my life to bring me joy and happiness."

"I have the power to create my reality."

"I now step out of my comfort zone to become the person I've always wanted to be."

"I attract people that support me."

"I choose to live my best life."

"I attract people that help me grow."

"I adapt well to the changes I am making."

CHAPTER 4:

HABITS FOR WEALTH

Many people dream of wealth. Many of us also wonder why we haven't achieved this goal. We work hard every day, so where is the wealth and luxurious lifestyle we dream of? The only tried, tested and true way to earn money is to provide a valuable service or product to others. It's that simple. Money isn't just for lucky people, it's for people that have a plan and work hard on their plan every day! It may not look like rich people work hard but this is because they have the privilege of having people and systems in place working for them. They can leverage their own time by having others do the work for them. But for most of us, we've got a ways to go before we can employ others to do our work for us.

In order to create the financial life that you've always dreamt of, you need only 2 things, a goal and a plan. And good old-fashioned hard work of course. Riches most effectively come to you if you can name an exact amount and then make your plan to get it.

If your goal is $10,000, or more, or less. You can have it! You just need a plan. Here are some ideas:

GOAL: $10,000

PLAN OPTIONS:
*Build and sell, 100 wooden coffee tables and sell them for 100$ each.
*Start a YouTube channel and learn about monetizing your video(s).
*Start a business doing what you are passionate about. Example: selling original artwork. You could sell 200 prints at 50$ each (minus expenses).
*Provide a valuable service. Perhaps a delivery service or yard care.

Make a vision board and use color and sparkles to super-charge your brain. Put "$10,000" on your board, put pictures of the things you will buy and do with the money, and also put pictures of the work that you will do to earn this money.

There are endless options and the right one for you should be based on what you enjoy. Then when tough times arise, as they always will. You will be more positive, resilient and quickly be able to pick yourself up and carry on. Think about the traveling analogy, if/when your car breaks down: if you are really excited about where you are going, you will get it fixed quickly and get back on your journey, if you are not excited about your destination, you might sit around for a while and use the car problem as an excuse to stall on your path to your goals.

Once you start earning extra income to reach your lifestyle goals, it is just important to keep that money. Let's have look at some bad wealth habits and some good ones that we can replace them with.

Old Bad Habits

Wasting time. You don't have to look far to find time wasters, social media and TV probably top the list. There is so much available to us via streaming or regular broadcasting, you might not realize this is a huge time waster. Do something that involves sharpening your brain, increasing the health of your body, or spend time executing or strategizing your plans for wealth.

Not keeping track of spending. It is very easy to lose track of where all that hard-earned money goes. A few fancy coffee drinks per week adds up to a lot of money. Money that could be spent paying down your credit cards or put towards your future.

Shopping sales or impulse buys. Some people just can't help buying something that is on sale. I personally know a few. They will come home stocked up with things they never needed in the first place because it was on sale.

Not saving. Try to save 10-20% of your income for your future. Get a separate bank account and sock it away there. If this doesn't work, you can put actual bills somewhere you won't be able to easily access them. You can also buy silver or gold coins or bars. These will go up in value and are not as easily spent as regular currency.

Relying on one stream of income. We have all seen in recent years how quickly things can change and you can be left with no job overnight. Try to start up a side-gig of sorts. Providing a valuable product or a service to others will guarantee some extra income.

Procrastinating. This is one of the most common and most crippling bad habits! The time is now, make a to-do list and work at checking those things off.

Not focussing. Set some big money goals, you can use my free "Creating A Vision Board" book and I would recommend my book "365 Days of Positive Affirmations" to help you find out what you really want in life. You need to feed your desire for riches and make it so strong that wealth has no choice but to come to you.

Giving up. Many people give up on their plans and goals when they haven't even given them a fair chance. The thing is, you can never tell how far you are from reaching your goal. It could be a ways off or it could be just around the corner. So don't quit! Your goals and dreams are closer than you might think.

New Good Habits

Provide a valuable product or service. As discussed earlier, this is the only sustainable way to riches. Keep brainstorming practical ideas for you. Find side-gigs that use your gifts and talents to provide a valuable product or service to others.

Being an early riser. It's hard to be productive when you don't start your day early. This is why nearly half of the self-made millionaires get out at least 3 hours before their 9-5 starts. This helps them tackle personal projects or plan for what will come next with a clear head, free from distractions like email notifications popping up onscreen while working. Also, when you wake up at the crack of dawn, it gives you a sense of power over your life. You're in control and can tackle anything that comes along with this newfound good habit.

Practicing gratitude daily. Being grateful for the things you have brings more of the things you want into your life. You can use my book "One Year of Gratitude Journaling" or just write down what you are grateful for on a piece of paper daily.

The best sleep is before midnight. This goes hand in hand with getting up early. My grandfather from the Old country in Europe used to say the best sleep is before midnight. He was right, your circadian rhythm wants you to sleep when it's dark and get up at the crack of dawn. Try to incorporate this good habit to increase your productivity.

Building multiple streams of income. Most of us have a 9-5 job. Whether we love it, hate it, or somewhere in the middle, relying solely on one income stream is a dicey way to go. As evidenced in the last few years, things can change quickly. Prepare today so that if your primary source of income disappears you will have a backup plan. You can provide a valuable product or service to others, start up a YouTube channel or start a business doing a hobby that you love. Brainstorm to find something that you enjoy that can also earn you money.

Setting priorities. Most of us do not have any priorities. Setting goals is a great way to motivate yourself, but it's hard if you don't know where your money should go or how much is enough for any given goal. Using your finances, you can invest in your future. What are your priorities? Retiring early? Saving to put your kids through college? Traveling the world? Add some photos that represent these things to your vision board. We all have different priorities, and we need financial planning tools to help sometimes. There are also personal planners for hire and Apps to give you some advice.

Saving and then spending. You should start your month by securing savings and investments - at least 20% of what you make. Spend from what is left. Warren Buffett once said, "Save First, Spend Later". It makes perfect sense if you don't want to be left with nothing at the end of your month.

Investing. Maintaining a monthly investment contribution is necessary to grow wealth, especially if other debts or expenses are coming up. So, the first step towards building healthy finances is to make sure you're continuously investing wisely each month. Set money aside in a retirement fund, buy safe securities on the stock market or get advice from a trusted financial planner.

Managing your time. A day has only 24 hours. If you're looking for success, then it's essential to understand how much time each task will take. Whether you want more money in your pocket or just some extra cash, you must utilize your resources efficiently and effectively and not waste any time. To have a productive day, keep your focus on the tasks at hand by making lists, and checking them off as completed or undone and prioritize based on importance. Using online tools may also help. If you need to, buy an analog clock or an old-school wristwatch so that you can see the second ticking by. Get to work now!

Building your team. On your road to wealth and success, you will need many people to help you along the way. And they are worth their weight in gold. The person that does some of your behind-the-scenes work for you, the person that encourages you to keep going, or the person at the shop that gives a good deal on supplies. Treat your team well, they are invaluable. People are more likely to help you if they feel like a valued member of your team. A respectful attitude towards others attracts opportunities that can turn into cash, so stay humble and be grateful.

Avoiding late fees. Automate your bill payments. Don't let late payments ruin your finances. Avoid these expensive mistakes by automating every bill with apps available today so you never have to worry about them again. It will help you get closer to achieving your goals quickly, while saving money along the way.

Making a list for expenditures. Creating a list and sticking by it can help you avoid impulse buys or picking up items that may not be necessary. Having an idea of what you need on your shopping trips will help you stay focused and not distracted by sales. Buying online can be a fantastic way to save money as well. You'll quickly get a sense of what you need and how much it will cost to buy. When making purchases online, wait at least 24 hours before committing. You may change your mind. As important as it is to earn the amount of money that you have been dreaming about, it is just as important to keep it.

Starting retirement plans as early as possible. An individual must plan if they want their life after their working years (or decades) to be filled with happiness and joy. Invest wisely because there have been some real bumps along the way, financially speaking, in the last few years. One way to prepare for retirement is by investing in physical assets, like real estate. Not only will this give you passive income from rent, but it could also be an attractive long-term investment opportunity with low risk.

A bonus tip: Take care of your health. As the old adage goes, "if wealth is lost, something is lost, but if health is lost, everything is lost". In the next chapter, you will learn about creating some good habits for maintaining health and promoting healing.

Positive Affirmations for Wealth

"Wealth is drawn to me like a magnet."

"Having enough money for everything I want is normal for me."

"Money comes to me quickly and easily."

"I give valuable services or products in exchange for money."

"Prosperity and success come naturally to me."

"I attract the riches that I desire."

"The money I spend goes to valuable places and comes back to me multiplied."

"I am always increasing my income."

"I am always thinking of new ways to earn money."

"I am good at managing my finances and easily reach my financial goals."

"I am a money magnet."

"Money comes to me in unexpected ways."

"I have an unlimited source of income in my life."

CHAPTER 5:

HABITS FOR HEALTH AND HEALING

Lifestyle changes fall into three categories:

- Behavioral: planning activities, sleeping habits, and physical activity
- Dietary: water intake and a nutritious diet
- Psychological: attitude, mood, and stress management

By simply incorporating some new habits into your daily routine, you can create personal health like never before. If you want to replace a bad habit routine with a healthy new one, use Template 5 to help you get started. Let's discuss a few essential habit changes here.

Old Bad Habits

Giving in to laziness. We all feel tired at the end of a long workday. Resting at the right time is important, but don't be deceived, physical exercise is the trick to getting more energy. It is also the best way to heal your body and maintain your body as you age. When we exercise so many great things happen, your body is filled with oxygen, (which has been linked to preventing diseases including cancer), it boosts your metabolism to help control an ideal weight, it promotes your sleep, increases your mood, it can be fun and many other benefits. The more you do it, the easier and more enjoyable it will get. So don't get sucked into your couch after a long day of work, go for a short walk!

Eating sugar. Refined sugar is maybe the worst invention in modern history. It can lead to diabetes, cancer and a multitude of other morbid illnesses. It also stimulates the same part of the brain as many drugs and has been shown to be more addictive than cocaine! Sugar affects our cognitive skills and also our self-control. The addiction-like effects caused by sugar can cause, over-eating, loss of self-control and even memory loss. Processed food contains a ton of refined sugar! Try to become more aware of what you are eating by reading the ingredients lists on the food you buy. If you have a sweet tooth already, try eating all kinds of fruit! The sugar in fruit is completely different from white or refined sugar, so try to find some different kinds of fruit that you enjoy!

Living under stress. Many of us have been under stress for so long that we don't know life to be any different. Some symptoms of too much stress in your life are insomnia, low energy, depression, acne, headaches, chronic pain, frequent illness, digestive issues and weight gain to name a few. Sound familiar? Some new habits include: getting enough sleep, exercising, eliminating stressors, lowering your caffeine and sugar intake, finding like-minded positive people to be around, meditation and deep breathing exercises.

Not giving your body what it needs. Your body wants to be healthy and heal. It is yearning for exercise and good food. Try to spend some time alone to listen to what your individual body needs and give it to yourself!

Taking drugs or alcohol. Putting any of these things in our bodies is not healthy, but in moderation, can reduce stress and cause enjoyment for some people. Substance use can be mild and recreational or become a more serious dependency. When the use becomes overpowering in a way that harms you or leads you to harm others like your family or friends in some way, then it is problematic. You will need to seek professional help to overcome this condition.

Over-eating. There is a Confucian teaching called Hara hachi bun me, which means eat until you are 80% full. It originated in Okinawa, Japan as a way to control eating habits. Okinawans interestingly have one of the lowest rates of illness from cancer, heart disease and stroke. Also, slow down when you're eating to give your body a chance to register how much you have eaten. Eating until you are "80% satisfied" instead of "full" has numerous health benefits. If you struggle with under-eating try to eat small portions more often, and seek professional help if you need to.

Smoking. Unfortunately, many people get hooked on this one when they are young and as the years go by it gets harder and harder to stop. You might need professional help to stop smoking and replace it with a healthy habit that includes some irresistible healthy rewards. Medical doctors can prescribe medication that can help, deep breathing and exercise have also been shown to be effective in combatting this bad habit.

New Good Habits

Getting quality Sleep. The correct amount of sleep can make a world of difference. A lack of good sound sleep affects the way your brain works, which in turn causes more problems. Getting enough sleep can help you protect not only mental but also physical health. Sleep helps the body regenerate, increases healthy brain function and maintains overall wellbeing. You must try to go to sleep at the same time every day. Keep your sleep schedule consistent on weeknights and weekends. Keep the bedroom dark, and don't watch TV or use screens before bedtime as they may signal your brain that it's time for action. Again, the old saying "The best sleep is before midnight" holds true today. Our body's circadian rhythm is dependant on light, so go to bed early and get up when the sun rises.

Moving and getting exercise. Optimum health cannot be achieved without physically moving around. A sedentary life has been linked to health problems like weight gain and heart disease. Be active, preferably for at least 30 minutes a day, every day to achieve your fitness goals. Evening walking or light jogging is a good starting habit to create. Not only that but those who are more physically engaged live longer too. If you currently do not exercise, start by doing some just once or twice per week at first, and gradually build longer routines up over time. There are so many kinds of enjoyable exercise to choose from, walking, running, swimming, weight lifting, rock climbing, dancing, yoga, aerobics, to name a few.

Cleaning your living space. If you are trying to kick a pesky bad habit and are not sure what to replace it with, cleaning your living environment is a fantastic habit to form and has numerous benefits. You can get great exercise from cleaning, it has a calming effect on your mind and it makes you feel happy to live in a clean environment.

Getting outside. Any kind of exercises are great habits to form, but there is something about being outside in nature, that has an extra deep calming effect. Sitting in nature can also help you to listen to your inner voice and figure out what makes you happy and what your long-term goals are. Fresh air and oxygen are essential for health and healing.

Drinking more water. The benefits to drinking more water are endless, this is a habit that you'll want to do multiple times in a day. Drinking more water has been shown to stabilize your heartbeat, regulate blood pressure, cushion your joints, aid in digestion, add energy and a ton of others benefits. Most adults need about 4-6 cups a day, around a liter. It is possible to drink too much water if you have certain health conditions including thyroid, kidney, liver, or heart problems or if you take some medications such as non-steroidal anti-inflammatory drugs (NSAIDs). Consult a doctor about water intake if you have a serious condition. But for most people, more water is the way to go!

Practicing good dietary habits. Eat more fruits and veggies for a healthy digestive system. Fruits and vegetables are rich in antioxidants, and contain fiber that helps you feel full longer, keeping your appetite under control. That's why the American Heart Association recommends filling at least half your plate with fruits or veggies every day so you can reach 4 ½ cups per day total! You can choose: canned, fresh, or frozen vegetables as they all count toward meeting this goal. Researchers have found a diet high in fruit and vegetables is capable of protecting against cancer, diabetes, and heart disease. Don't eat junk food and try to cut back on processed foods. Making smoothies is a great daily habit that easily incorporates more fruits and veggies into your diet.

Relaxing. Take out time for yourself. You can't give your all to everything if you're not taking care of yourself. Self-care should be refreshing and calming. Focusing on self-care will help make sure you don't burn out. Try to maintain good habits such as exercising regularly. Meditation, yoga, exercise, reading and many others can also be relaxing positive habits.

Putting limits on social media. Do not let social media take the better part of your life. Limit your time exposure on social media. Try to make rules like "no phones in the bedroom, after dinner time" etc., to help implement keeping away from social media. Or you can change "My Phone Settings" by going into Settings > Screen Time and restricting usage for apps during certain hours so that there is downtime each day. Small things go a long way. Try it out.

Being Disciplined. There is nothing more important than discipline when trying to create optimum personal health. Eating the right food and exercising can be vital to living a healthy lifestyle. But if you're not disciplined, it's all for nothing, no matter what type of diet or exercise routine you choose. To improve your health, change your mindset. A lack of discipline makes achieving long-term goals nearly impossible. Any successful habit requires a consistent investment of your time and effort. Use your vision board, positive affirmations and the templates in Chapter 10, to help keep you on track when forming your new habits.

Doing Crossword Puzzles. Long before Alzheimer's or Dementia became an issue, researchers found that mentally challenging activities may offer protection against the risk of these diseases. Playing games like chess and solving puzzles regularly, as well as, engaging your mind with reading can help lower chances in those prone to develop these conditions. Though there is no cure yet, prevention through different methods such as eating certain foods ensures less likelihood of cognitive decline later down the line. Staying socially engaged has proven to be beneficial as well.

Giving your body what it needs. Your body wants to be healthy and heal. Take some time to get to know your own mind and body and provide it with the nutrients and exercise needed for your specific body and mind.

Take vitamins and supplements. This is a great daily habit. It is insurance for nutrients that may be lacking in your diet.

Resting when you need to. There is a big difference between resting and being lazy. You need to figure out how much rest you need as an individual and stick to that routine. Then it will be easier to tell if you're being swept into a lazy routine or if you actually need a rest. Many of us can use a power nap, or a short rest during the day in addition to a good night's sleep. So figure out how long you need to effectively recharge and then get back to doing something productive. Don't get trapped by your favorite streaming App!

Positive Affirmations for Health and Healing

"My body is healthy and full of energy."

"I only eat healthy food and give my body everything it needs to heal."

"I love getting exercise and always look for new enjoyable ways to exercise."

"I feel strong and fit."

"I listen to my body and give it what it needs."

"I feel healing energy all around me."

"The more I exercise, the more energy I get."

"I am only interested in things that serve my health."

"I forgive myself and others."

"I love my body and it serves me well."

"I am full of energy."

"I am in the process of healing."

"I allow myself to heal."

"I am creating inner peace."

"I am grateful for my body."

CHAPTER 6:

HABITS FOR LOVE AND MEANINGFUL HUMAN CONNECTION

What is love? This is the big question, there are even songs written about it. It is different for everyone. Primarily, most people think of love as attracting your soulmate and living happily ever after. This is a fantastic goal but it is just one small part of the love you need in your life. Love with a partner is very important, but so is self-love, career love and loving connections with others in your life.

The Ancient Greeks had 6 different words for 6 different kinds of love. Philia, (deep friendship), Ludus (playful love), Agape (love for everyone), Pragma (longstanding love), Philautia (love of the self) and Eros (sexual passion). And research has found that between all the world's languages there is a total of 14 different kinds of love! So if you're stalled in finding your soulmate, don't give up, but know that there are many kinds of love to fulfill feelings of loneliness, or the need for meaningful human connection.

In order to change your relationships for the better, you will have to change some of your habits. Many people believe that to create love in their life, they need to change their entire lifestyle, luckily, this isn't true. Here are some habit changes that will add up over time. Let's look at some destructive habits holding us back and see if we can replace them with some more positive productive ones.

Old Bad Habits

Not listening to others. Most people hear but don't listen. Some of the reasons why we don't listen are, our natural desire to talk, our instinct to judge others, you may have preconceptions or biases, your ego is getting in the way or you're just not interested and thinking about something else. Try to think about being respectful to everyone. Truly listening to them shows respect, whereas not paying attention or listening is disrespectful.

Focussing on the negatives. You may have friends that you mutually complain with, but for the most part, this is an unattractive quality when meeting new people and beginning new relationships of any kind. Try to be aware of your words. Instead of talking about some negative, destructive current event, find something positive and uplifting to talk about.

Talking and not doing. Many people are all talk and no action. Why? Because talking is easier than doing. Become aware of how much you talk and how much of it translates to action.

Not being open-minded. You may write off a wonderful person/friendship or acquaintance because you have preconceived notions about them. Try to let their actions form your opinion about them. You might be surprised.

Pointing fingers and blaming others. This is a bad habit that many people do without being aware of it. When something goes wrong they quickly jump to blame or point a finger at someone else. Whether or not you are responsible for the problem, don't be quick to accuse others. Eventually, you can figure out why the thing happened, who is responsible and how to avoid it next time. But make sure you have the facts first before jumping to conclusions.

Not being vulnerable and putting yourself out there. Nobody wants to get their heart broken or be disappointed with friendships. This is a big deterrent for many people in seeking new relationships of any kind. A lot of it has to do with expectations. It is a great idea to make of list of the qualities you want to find in another person, but when you meet someone new don't expect them to be the person with all those qualities. You might need to meet a large number of people in order to find friends and partners that are compatible with you. Many times we think the first person we meet is "the one" when the chances of that being true are slim to none. Don't expect much from new acquaintances, take time to see if it is someone that fits and complements your lifestyle and goals for the future.

Judging others. Don't be quick to judge others, they might have other things going on in their lives than you can readily see. You might lose out on a great relationship because you have created negative thoughts about them for no good reason. Try to be compassionate, when others do something that makes you raise your eyebrow, try to see their side of it as well.

New Good Habits

Visualizing your future. It's important to know exactly what you want in your life. What does your perfect life look like? Having money and a nice home or traveling around constantly with no responsibilities whatsoever? What kinds of relationships do you want to create in your life? The clearer your vision, the faster and more easily you can create an amazing life full of love. Download my free book "Creating a Vision Board" to help you get started.

Being a good listener. Listening is an art and a skill. Sometimes it's not easy, but it's worth working on because people will appreciate your efforts. So listen more than you speak. This quality makes you a lovable person, as it helps others feel seen and understood and makes them want to tell their story so they can be heard. This creates a fantastic feeling of connection between two individuals.

Being empathetic. It's not enough to be kind. We must understand and appreciate others as well. The more empathy one has with others' feelings, thoughts, or emotions, the better their ability to communicate difficult things. Try to walk in other's shoes, offer kindness to others and if you disagree about something, don't turn it into a debate.

Practicing mindfulness. It is easier to understand other people's perspectives when you're more present and aware of what is going on around you. Try looking at things from different angles. If this had happened to me, how would I have handled it? And "how would I feel if I were in their position? Being open-minded is very important when meeting new people. Your preconceptions or bias can get in the way and stop a fantastic friendship before it even gets started. Try not to judge or overreact when interacting with others.

Developing compassion. Sometimes it's not easy to find compassion in a world that seems to be full of negativity. However, by simply making a few small changes in how you think and act, you can become a more compassionate person. First, try to develop self-compassion and become more understanding and patient with yourself. Meditation might help, try to let all that judgment go out of you like an open window and then practice kindness towards others.

Never stop learning. Take some time for your hobbies and passions in life. Learning new things will help build up those happy brain cells which have an effect on our relationships. From how we act at our jobs to socializing with friends, learning new things will have a positive effect. Your brain will have more energy because it's engaged with what interests you and you will be interesting to talk to when meeting new people.

Treating everyone with respect. If you can take time out of your day to say "hello" as you pass by others, this will not only have a positive effect on you but also improve how they see themselves. Treating those around us with respect will ensure that good energy comes back to us as well. Treating people well will create smiles which can translate into love and happiness for all involved.

Listening to your instincts. Spend some time daily to get to know yourself and to listen to your inner voice. If you haven't been listening for a while, it will take some time before you hear it again. It will tell you all you need to know for your future dreams and goals and how to get there. Use Template 1 in Chapter 10 to get to know yourself and start listening to your inner voice and learn about your likes and dislikes. Eventually, your instincts will be spot on and you will trust them.

Loving yourself. You are all you have, so take care of yourself! Simply put, self-love is the assurance that your needs will be met and you will do whatever it takes to keep yourself healthy. Self-care means making sure all parts of oneself are taken care of, not just physical needs but also mental and emotional wellbeing as well.

Positive Affirmations for Love and Meaningful Human Connection

"I attract love from others because I love myself first."

"I radiate love to everyone I meet."

"I am a good person and am worthy of love."

"I am worthy of fulfilling relationships."

"I forgive myself for my past mistakes."

"I am grateful for the love I receive."

"I attract loving and trusting relationships."

"The Universe surrounds me with love."

"I love myself and others unconditionally."

"I find meaning and connection in many relationships."

"I practice listening and not speaking with everyone I meet."

CHAPTER 7:

HABITS FOR HAPPINESS

Happiness is different for everyone and it consists of all the topics in this book. It is the perfect blend, custom-made for your life. The things needed for your happiness are unique to only you. For some of us and at different stages in our life, sometimes we just don't know what would make us happy.

Use Template 1 in Chapter 10 to get an idea of what your subconscious true self is yearning for. If you have not yet made a vision board, get some magazines or newspapers, have a look through them and don't question what you are attracted to, just cut it out. It could be a new couch, a tranquil garden with a cup of tea, a sailing ship, a mountain, a forest, or a new car. Whatever you are attracted to cut it out and make an additional vision board if you have already made one. Keep it in a place where you can look at it multiple times throughout the day. Use the positive affirmations at the end of this chapter when you look at your vision board.

Good daily habits are the key to happiness. If we can identify what is causing the gloom and break those behavioral routines, you will be happier in your daily life.

Old Bad Habits

Procrastinating. Postponing or delaying a task or set of tasks is procrastination. Sometimes the longer you delay will cause negative consequences. This is a common habit that many people do without even knowing it. Make a to-do list and get to work now!

Not knowing yourself. How can you expect to find happiness if you don't know what makes you happy? Spend some time each day by yourself listening to your inner self and feeling what it is you want to accomplish in your life. Creating a vision board by going through magazines and cutting out photos of what you are attracted to, can help you learn what makes you happy. It can be a simple as a color that you enjoy and need more of in your home, it could be a new car or a new meaningful relationship. Spend some time setting some goals for achieving things that truly make you happy.

Not following your dreams. Dream big. After you have created your vision board of your big goals and the things that will truly bring you happiness, it's time to make a plan to get there. Using my book "365 days of Positive Affirmations", will help you reach your goals. Visualizations, affirmations, big goals and solid consistent plans to achieve them will ensure that you reach your dreams and live your best life.

Not setting goals. Many people go through life without any goals for the future. Please don't be one of them. We only have a short time on this earth to live up to our full potential. But it doesn't just happen. You need to set some goals and work at them to achieve the life you've dreamed of.

Not following your plan. It is worth it to spend some time making a solid plan to reach your goals. It can be a business plan or a list of affirmations and a vision board. After you've done all this hard work, don't stop! You are just getting started, many times people have great plans but they fail to follow through on them. Following your plan consistently and focussing will get you to your goals. Your plan is the yellow brick road to your dreams!

Holding grudges. I'll admit this is a tough one for me. If someone wrongs you or treats you badly, it is natural to respond by thinking of that person negatively and not wanting to be open with them again. Holding on to anger, bitterness and resentment has been shown to harm YOU and not just the person you direct your feelings towards. Rumination occurs when you think regularly about the person that wronged you and what occurred, this keeps us stuck and in a negative frame of mind. Harboring negative feelings is bad for you! If the person is important to you and has apologized, asked for forgiveness, and/or realized they have hurt you, then forgiving and accepting is a good option for you. If the person in question doesn't feel like they've done anything wrong, then your only option is to distance yourself from them "let it go", and get on with your life. If someone won't accept what they have done you can always thank them in your mind FOR GIVING you that experience and what you have learned from it and choose to minimally associate with that person. Try to forgive, but not forget. Move on with your life but don't give that person another chance to mistreat you.

New Good Habits

Maintaining your mental health. Happiness emanates from your mind. So, it's not just about what you do physically, but also mentally. Try to take care of how you feel inside and try to eliminate bad habits. You may think this sounds hard, but it takes only a few minutes per day. So set aside some time today to focus solely on improving your mood and developing a grateful, positive attitude.

Being grateful. Develop an attitude of gratitude. Being grateful for what you already have in your life will help attract more of what you want. You can use my Journal, "One Year of Gratitude Journaling" to help develop a grateful attitude and attract abundance into your life. Remember, when you have a grateful attitude you are living in grace, you will be attuned to the Universe and good things will continue to happen for you!

Getting to know yourself. This might be the ultimate key to happiness. Sadly, many of us become adults and don't know what makes us happy. It starts when you're young and you are unable to follow your dreams and the things that you enjoy. So that part of your inner voice gets turned off. Take some time each day to listen and cultivate your inner voice, it will tell you exactly what you need to be happy and fulfilled in your life!

Exercising regularly. You might think that exercise is just about the physical act of movement, but it's so much more than that. It can be mental, spiritual, and emotional as well! A little effort goes a long way, even if it's only 10 minutes at lunchtime or before bed each night. Exercise has been found to be beneficial in reducing symptoms of depression and boost happiness levels for some people. You could choose activities like running marathons or scaling cliffs. The trick isn't exercising until exhaustion sets in, but instead finding an activity that makes your heart sing without feeling overly challenging. Walking, a yoga class, a swim or a bike ride are all great activities to get started.

Accepting challenges and learning from them. Sometimes things come up that we didn't plan for, it is just a part of life. If you can see the silver lining in the clouds of challenge that arise, you will be able to learn something important and continue your journey to your goals that much wiser and more prepared for next time. When things go wrong, take care of yourself, try a deep breathing exercise, or spending some quality one-on-one time with friends/family members who love you. You can learn just as much from challenges and mistakes as you can from a success.

Facing stress. Stress is universal, and it can be a good thing. Stress helps us when we need to lift weights, for example. What matters most in life (and our health) is how one handles stressful events. Shifting your perspective on stressful issues will make them seem less daunting, and you might even find a bright side. Make a list of what needs to be done and go through the tasks one by one. A sense of humor can keep things light-hearted when needed as well. Positive affirmations like "I can manage everything" will help you feel less stressed when there is a lot that needs to be done.

Decluttering. Decluttering works like therapeutic medicine. For the next 20 minutes, can you set aside time to tidy up and pass some things on to others? Particularly, those areas in your home where things are all over and out-of-sorts. It takes only a few minutes a day to keep your home clutter-free. There are books written with tips and advice to help you as well.

Practicing mindfulness. Living in the present moment is a life-changing experience, and you can have the most happiness by being in the NOW. Try to go through the day without judging and/or overreacting to anything. Try to be mindful of where each day takes us, and trust that you are on your right path, regardless of what comes up. Walk, take breaks, share laughter or check mindfulness Apps.

Forgetting about your phone. The electronics world has been moving at a rapid pace, and it's easy to get caught up in that realm. Instead of sitting on social media scrolling through hours' worth of posts while eating, turn off your gadgets for at least an hour once a week and you'll be surprised by all the changes this makes. You can read, meditate or take a walk.

Smiling more. A study showed how smiling could make people happier, scowling angrier and frowning sadder. Smiling is good for your brain! When you smile, tiny molecules in our brains called neuropeptides are released, which helps fight off stress. Then other neurotransmitters like dopamine or serotonin come into play too! The best way to recover from a mental illness may be an easy smile. A recent study has found that forcing people who suffer from depression or anxiety disorders into smiling can provide them with some joy.

Meeting friends. If you're feeling lonely, reach out to your friends. A friend is the best remedy for a blue mood. It can feel like an uphill battle to make new friends and create meaningful relationships in adulthood, but that doesn't mean you should give up. Spend time with one or two people in particular whom you enjoy being around with nothing particularly exciting is happening. These friendships will remain strong because both parties care for each other when things aren't so busy. Friends of friends are also a fantastic way to meet new people.

Positive Affirmations for Happiness

"I am worthy of being happy."

"I accept myself unconditionally."

"I am proud of myself."

"I am creating the life I've always wanted."

"I allow myself to be happy now."

"I create my own happiness and joy."

"I expand my inner joy by sharing it with others."

"I have everything I need to be happy now."

"I am on the path to my goals and am enjoying the journey."

"I choose happiness."

"Everything is going to be ok."

"The timing in my life is perfect and everything is falling into place perfectly."

CHAPTER 8:

HABITS FOR SELF-CONFIDENCE AND SELF-ESTEEM

Self-confidence is a feeling about your own skills and abilities. Having self-confidence means you trust yourself and feel in control of your life. Self-esteem is an evaluation of your own worth. Self-esteem includes beliefs about yourself as well as emotional states and feelings. In order to build these in yourself, you first have to get to know yourself. You also need a record of making good choices for yourself. This is how your confidence and esteem will grow. Continuing with bad habits will lower your self-confidence and self-esteem while switching to some good and productive habits will increase these in yourself.

Old Bad Habits

Not knowing yourself. Spend some time each day getting to know YOU. This might sound odd since you might be a full-grown adult for many years now but trust me it's not. A huge number of people go through life not truly knowing their likes and dislikes and therefore can never be truly happy. Use the template in Chapter 10, to brainstorm some ideas about your likes and dislikes. By making choices based on your likes and dislikes, you will be happy with yourself and learn to trust yourself. Your self-confidence and self-esteem will grow and true happiness will find you.

Caring more about others than you do about yourself. This can mean pouring your energy into caring for others and not yourself, or it can mean caring about what others think about you more than your own feelings about yourself. Use affirmations to turn off the chatter in your brain, it only matters what you think about yourself. If you spend too much time caring for others, you might not have an option to stop immediately, but try to prioritize your own needs. Make time for yourself. Remember the famous airplane analogy, you have to put on your own oxygen mask before you can help others.

Not following your dreams. Many of us don't even have big dreams and goals. I encourage you to create a vision board and learn about yourself and your dreams for the future. Once you have identified them, you can make your plan and work every day on fulfilling your big dreams.

Caring about what others think. The need to be accepted is a strong human need. But sometimes it can become overwhelmming and consume our thoughts and actions. Quite often when this need becomes overwhelming it has to do with trauma from the past. If you grew up in an emotionally distant household, you might always be striving for comments about acceptance from others. There are also many other scenarios that can result in over-caring about what others think. Some ideas for overcoming this consuming need/bad habit are, to let go of perfection (however it turns out is just fine), get to know yourself more, find your tribe/like-minded people and become your own friend. Make a long list of positive affirmations and use them daily to help you get over this habit.

Feeling like others hold power over you. Some of us suffer from this bad habit and it is a perpetual loop. Often someone we care about can have a negative influence over some part of our life. To start combatting this feeling, you have to establish healthy boundaries and take responsibility for your own emotions, NOT theirs. It could be as simple as a friend always complaining to you and you don't want to hear about it anymore. Once you establish some boundaries with them, they may react in an uncomfortable way. This is their problem, not yours. Or your issue could be more serious, a spouse or parent that exerts a negative influence over you multiple times in a day. Try to spend more time away from this person and gradually set up boundaries. You may never be able to change this person but you can change yourself, and remember their reactions are about them, not you. Use deep breathing, positive self-talk and positive affirmations to help you get through.

Not being brave and courageous. Positive affirmations will help here. And doing a 180 to replace this habit of lacking courage. Tell yourself "I am brave, I am strong." over and over. Write it on your wall and set reminders on your smartphone. Bravery is a muscle, the more you do it, the easier it will get. Just imagine your self-esteem growing when you've done something courageous that you can be proud of.

Not trusting your instincts. If you are trapped in a negative relationship of any kind, you might not hear your own instincts anymore. But they are still there. Take a pencil and a paper or use the notes App on your smartphone, go for a walk and sit quietly somewhere. It will take some time to hear your instincts loudly, when you do, write them down so that you don't forget. Take action toward following your instincts.

Not doing what you said you would do. This is a habit that makes others think you can't be trusted but it also makes yourself think that you can't trust yourself. If you promise your body exercise and good food and then don't follow through, your inner voice and your actions are disconnected and you will never reach your goals. Not only that but you are undermining your instincts. Instincts get stronger when you act on them. Following through on your words shows yourself and others that you are a person of integrity and can be trusted.

New Good Habits

Following your dreams. If you have created a vision board of the things you would like for your future, now is the time to make some plans to get there! Your plan is the yellow brick road to your dreams and goals. Spend some time making a good solid plan and get to work every day until you reach each goal.

Spending quiet time with yourself. Learn your values and what is important to you. Meditating, going for a walk, drawing, knitting, exercising, or just sitting in nature will help you listen to your inner voice. Many people look to the outside world for all the answers to having a good life but the answers are inside you. Cultivate your inner voice, listening to it is a great daily habit.

Working on your bravery muscles. The more often you exhibit bravery and courage, the easier it will become. Visualize yourself being brave in certain difficult situations and use positive affirmations to help you develop your bravery and courage. "I am brave, I am courageous" are great daily affirmations.

Believing in yourself. Self-confidence is a powerful thing. It can propel you to accomplish your goals and dreams, or it could hold back all progress for fear of failure. Confident people aren't afraid of what will happen next in life because they have faith in themselves. Self-belief fuels their confidence which then sparks action even when faced with obstacles on the way. They trust themselves, maintain a positive outlook and talk positively to themselves.

Working on your determination. Self-confidence and self-esteem can be tough to build, but a big part of nurturing them is all in how we think. Having a positive, determined, unstoppable attitude about your dreams and goals, will ensure that you reach them. Use positive affirmations to develop your determination.

Don't let negative thoughts overpower you. An honest assessment of yourself and then taking action based on that awareness will go a long way. Stop preventing the things that you want by indulging in negative thoughts.

Instead of thinking about all the people who have better lives than yours, focus on one thing at a time and do something new every day to make yourself feel better. Use positive affirmations to change your thoughts when negatives creep in.

Dressing immaculately. You know that feeling of success, self-confidence, and poise you get when your outfit is just right? Wearing nice clothes makes a person feel like they can take on anything. Not everyone needs to dress up expensively or in designer wear, but if you can make efforts with your own personal style it will help create balance in your life. It has been said that one's mood depends on how one looks. Fake it until you make it!

Talking slowly. We all have that friend who speaks too quickly. They're always in a hurry and don't care if you understand them or not. They're no fun when we try to chat because their words just fly by too fast. Try listening to some influential people. They talk slow and take their time. They make sure every word is important, no matter how small it is. Even if you don't feel confident speaking slowly, try to practice, your voice will sound more professional than if you rush. People will feel respected and you will be successful in your conversation.

Gaining more knowledge. It is important to become more knowledgeable in order for you to feel confident. This includes learning and researching business opportunities, which will help build your confidence in many different areas. You can learn about any topic or subject matter under the sun. But make sure it is something interesting to you. Use the internet or observe people around you. You can use books and magazines to get information that might not be online or in your local library. Educational institutions also offer classes that will help with any goal you have.

Maintaining good posture. Slouching is bad for you, but sitting up straight could help protect your brain and make it function better. When you slouch, your lungs can't do their job. They're compromised and don't get the oxygen they need to function at full capacity, which means less air for other parts of the body like our brain. But when we sit up straight it may help us think better as well because staying calm has benefits beyond just being more relaxed physically; this feeling helps with confidence too.

Following through on your words. If you don't intend to do something, then don't say you're going to do it. Don't be known as the person that is all talk and no action. Show yourself and others that "you mean what you say, and say what you mean."

Embracing discomfort. You must trust yourself and step outside of your comfort zone to raise self-esteem. Confident people didn't become so in a day. The bulk of people are stuck inside their own personal bubbles and think they'll achieve greatness without taking any risks. Remember your thoughts create your reality. So use affirmations like "I am successful", when stepping outside of your comfort zone.

Positive Affirmations for Self-Confidence and Self-Esteem

"I believe in myself."

"I am proud of myself."

"I take steps every day to reach my ultimate dreams and goals."

"I make good choices."

"I am free."

"I am brave and courageous."

"I have big goals and work hard every day to achieve them."

"My skills and talents and valuable and will help me reach my goals."

"Every setback makes me wiser and stronger."

"How I feel about myself is most important."

"I deeply love and accept myself."

"I listen to my inner voice and trust what I hear."

"I can manage whatever comes my way."

"I am successful."

CHAPTER 9:

EXTREME HABITS:
ADDICTIONS, SUBSTANCE USE,
AND COMPULSIONS

If you suffer from one of these conditions, you will probably need professional help to stop them. Largely because these conditions cause your physical body to suffer, not only your mental health, and you will need multiple layers of support to successfully ditch these excessive habits that have turned into something else more serious. These conditions can start out harmlessly as a bad habit and quickly or slowly, over time turn into something that is out of control, harmful and can't be stopped by your willpower alone. Be sure to recognize if you need help and don't stop looking until you find it!

This book does not attempt to replace any medical or professional help, what it does is try to raise your awareness so that you can seek support if you need it.

Substance use and Addiction

Substance abuse is now commonly referred to as "substance use disorder" which is now a popular medical term for addiction. This encompasses both mild abuse and more severe dependence cases. "Addiction" usually refers to someone's behavior while "dependence" refers to physical symptoms of withdrawal and tolerance. Substance use can become the main priority of an addicted person, regardless of the harm it causes themselves or others. Addiction is marked by changes in behavior caused by biochemical changes in the brain as a result of continued substance use.

If you are suffering from a serious addiction, it can be complicated to change it. In my opinion only, addiction problems can start as a deeply ingrained extreme bad habit that eventually causes serious mental and/or physical problems. It is not as easy as picking a new positive habit to replace it with. Most countries have a government website about addiction and substance use which is a good place to start looking for some extra help. Your medical doctor can give you some direction as well. You will need support on many levels and in some cases medical assistance to deal with physical withdrawal-type symptoms.

When someone becomes addicted it might likely stem back to missing an important part of human connection during one's developmental years. This tends to result in a big empty, missing piece in one's life that can easily be filled with drugs or alcohol or in other cases things like food. A good first step in recovery is analyzing why you may have started the addiction that you suffer from. What void and pain were you trying to pacify? If you can start to understand the motivations in starting, you can get some ideas as to which habits would be the most successful in helping to replace your addiction.

I have long believed that those individuals that seem to have a predisposition for substance use or addictions also have to greatest capacity to love and to accomplish great things. Their energy is misdirected. Often, the only new habit that can replace an addiction is meaningful human connection. Volunteering, doing community outreach, or seeking a job where you can help others might be some options to consider. There is also evidence that caring for animals, gardening and deep breathing can help to overcome substance use conditions. As I said earlier, this won't be as easy to fix as a habit like biting your nails, and you will need many layers of support.

Smoking can also fall under substance use, smoking starts as a bad habit, but quickly your body becomes dependant on the various chemicals involved in smoking and your brain becomes dependent on the routine as well. Some people can kick this habit on their own, but many require professional help and support. A medical doctor can prescribe medication to help with the craving and you can replace the smoking routine with exercise, deep-breathing, chewing gum, having a candy sucker or anything else that you come up with that will work for you personally.

Compulsions and Obsessive-Compulsive Disorder.

Obsessive-Compulsive disorder is a mental illness that causes people to have recurring, unwanted thoughts, ideas, or sensations (obsessions), that make them feel driven to do something repetitively (compulsions). How can you tell if your habit is normal or has OCD characteristics? People that have OCD sometimes have thoughts or actions that: take up over an hour a day, aren't enjoyable, are beyond their control, interfere with work or social life, or another part of their life. Some types of OCD are, "checking" things like locks, "contamination" (worry about dirt, etc) and symmetry and ordering (lining things up again and again). Stress can make OCD worse and there is no cure, but doctors recommend cognitive psychotherapy, medication, relaxation as well as some other useful treatments. If you think you suffer from this disorder, please find a professional to help you.

Problem gambling is a compulsive disorder and can be harmful to psychological and physical health. It is classified as an impulse control disorder and a gambling addiction can lead to feelings of helplessness and despondency and people that live with this disorder might experience depression, anxiety, and other problems. If you suffer from problem gambling please seek professional help to get you to stop this compulsive disorder.

Eating habits.

Some eating disorders can be created as a result of bad eating habits. But they usually have a psychological component as well. Seek help if you suffer from over-eating or under-eating. There is support out there, you just have to find it and not give up until you do! A medical doctor or a government website is a good place to start.

Positive Affirmations to overcome Extreme Habits

"I replace my bad habits with good ones that benefit my mind and body."

"I only put good nutrients into my body."

"I take one day at a time,

"I take care of myself."

"I comfort myself."

"I am becoming the best version of myself."

"I like the person that I am becoming."

"I am on the right path now and I will not stop."

"The past is over, the future is bright."

"I am becoming stronger every day."

"I am strong and fearless."

"My addiction is strong, but my willpower is stronger."

"I attract positive, healthful, and productive things into my life every day."

"Amazing things are headed my way."

"I have a plan to overcome my extreme habit and I stick to it."

CHAPTER 10:

TEMPLATES FOR HABIT CHANGING

If you have bought the paperback version of this book, you can write directly in the templates or photocopy them for future use. If you have the ebook version, you will have to copy them yourself onto a blank piece of paper. Use the templates over and over again to help you replace bad habits and create new ones so you can reach your goals and dreams quickly and effectively!

Template 1: Getting to know yourself

Use his template to brainstorm about yourself. Don't judge yourself just make a list as long as you can of your likes and dislikes. Awareness of yourself is a great first step in identifying which habits you want to change to help you on your journey to your big goals.

Template 2: Habits to Change list

Use this template to make a list of the habits that you want to change in your life. You can add to it at any time. Try to go through one at a time and make a plan to change your habit using the ideas in Chapter 3. You might want to avoid the cue or change the habit routine.

Template 3: Individual Bad habit awareness and progress

Once you have picked a habit to change, use this template to get to know your habit and the history of why you started. Make a plan to start changing your habit.

Template 4: Avoiding the Cue

If your bad habit can be stopped by avoiding the cue. Use this sheet. Brainstorm some ideas to stay away from your cue. Come up with some phrases to tell people if your habit has a social basis.

Template 5: Replacing the Routine.

If you can't avoid the cue for your bad habit, you will have to replace the behavioral routine. Find a new routine to replace the old destructive routine.

Template 6: More Rewards.

Use this template when you have a particularly bad habit routine that you have a hard time giving up. Make the list of rewards as long as you need to, add in things that have nothing to do with your habit to help motivate you. Remember if you can keep it up for 2-3 months, the new routine will become automatic.

Template 7: Slip-up Awareness

Slip-ups are part of life. Two steps forward and one step back. When you have a moment and do your old habit routine, use this sheet to analyze how it happened and how you were feeling. Make a plan to prevent another slip-up (but if it happens, it's ok, be patient with yourself).

Template 8: Bad Habit Daily Progress

Keep track of how many times per day you do your bad habit, and work on reducing the frequency.

Template 9: List of Good Habits to cultivate

Use this template for general good habits that don't need to replace any bad routines. Drinking more water, eating more fruit are things we should all cultivate and remind ourselves to do daily. If you are not replacing a bad habit, your new habit will take around 21 days to become automatic.

Template 10: Good Habit Daily Progress

Keep track of how many times per day you do your bad habit, and work on reducing the frequency.

Template 1: Getting to know yourself

My likes (colors, people, places, things to do)

_____

_____

_____

_____

_____

_____

_____

_____

_____

_____

_____

My dislikes (colors, people, places, things to do)

_____

_____

_____

_____

_____

_____

_____

_____

_____

_____

_____

Template 1: Getting to know yourself

My likes (colors, people, places, things to do)

_____

_____

_____

_____

_____

_____

_____

_____

_____

_____

_____

_____

My dislikes (colors, people, places, things to do)

_____

_____

_____

_____

_____

_____

_____

_____

_____

_____

_____

_____

Template 2: Habits to Change list

Bad Habits that I want to change:

_____

_____

_____

_____

_____

_____

_____

_____

_____

_____

_____

Phrase these Habits positively:

_____

_____

_____

_____

_____

_____

_____

_____

_____

_____

Template 2: Habits to Change list

Bad Habits that I want to change:

_____

_____

_____

_____

_____

_____

_____

_____

_____

_____

_____

Phrase these Habits positively:

_____

_____

_____

_____

_____

_____

_____

_____

_____

_____

_____

Template 3:
Individual Bad Habit Awareness

Bad Habit that I want to change:

_____

_____

When did this habit start?

_____

_____

Who was I with?

_____

_____

How was I feeling?

_____

_____

Replacement routine ideas:

_____

_____

_____

_____

Positive Affirmations:

_____

_____

_____

_____

_____

_____

Template 3:
Individual Bad Habit Awareness

Bad Habit that I want to change:

_____

_____

When did this habit start?

_____

_____

Who was I with?

_____

_____

How was I feeling?

_____

_____

Replacement routine ideas:

_____

_____

_____

_____

_____

Positive Affirmations:

_____

_____

_____

_____

_____

_____

_____

Template 4: Avoiding the cue

Bad Habit that I want to change:

_____
_____
_____

What is the cue or trigger?

_____
_____

Time, place or person that is the cue/trigger:

_____
_____

Ways to avoid the cue:

_____
_____
_____
_____
_____

Phrases to tell someone to avoid a social routine:

_____
_____
_____
_____
_____

Template 4: Avoiding the cue

Bad Habit that I want to change:

_____

_____

_____

What is the cue or trigger?

_____

_____

Time, place or person that is the cue/trigger:

_____

_____

Ways to avoid the cue:

_____

_____

_____

_____

Phrases to tell someone to avoid a social routine:

_____

_____

_____

_____

_____

Template 5: Replacing the routine.

Bad Habit that I want to change:

_____
_____
_____

What is the behavioral routine?

_____
_____

Ideas to replace the routine:

_____
_____
_____

Benefits of the new routine:

_____
_____
_____
_____

Positive Affirmations to help with the new routine:

_____
_____
_____
_____
_____
_____

Template 5: Replacing the routine.

Bad Habit that I want to change:

_____
_____
_____

What is the behavioral routine?

_____
_____

Ideas to replace the routine:

_____
_____
_____

Benefits of the new routine:

_____
_____
_____
_____

Positive Affirmations to help with the new routine:

_____
_____
_____
_____
_____
_____

Template 6: More Rewards

Bad Habit that I want to change:

_____
_____
_____

Phrase it postively:

_____
_____

**Benefits of giving up the bad habit
and starting the new habit:**

_____
_____
_____
_____
_____

More benefits/rewards for extra motivation:

_____
_____
_____
_____
_____
_____
_____

Template 6: More Rewards

Bad Habit that I want to change:

_____

_____

_____

_____

Phrase it postively:

_____

_____

_____

**Benefits of giving up the bad habit
and starting the new habit:**

_____

_____

_____

_____

_____

_____

_____

More benefits/rewards for extra motivation:

_____

_____

_____

_____

_____

_____

_____

_____

Template 7: Slip-up Awareness

What happened?

_____

_____

Where was I?

_____

_____

How was I feeling?

_____

Who was I with?

_____

What can I do next time to avoid a slip-up?

_____

_____

_____

_____

Positive Affirmations to help staying on track:

_____

_____

_____

_____

_____

_____

Template 7: Slip-up Awareness

What happened?

_____

_____

Where was I?

_____

_____

How was I feeling?

_____

Who was I with?

_____

What can I do next time to avoid a slip-up?

_____

_____

_____

_____

Positive Affirmations to help staying on track:

_____

_____

_____

_____

_____

Template 8:
Individual Bad Habit Daily Progress

Bad Habit that I want to stop doing:

_____

Date:	How many times per day:

Template 8:
Individual Bad Habit Daily Progress

Bad Habit that I want to stop doing:

_____

_____

Date:	How many times per day:

Template 9: List of
Daily Good Habits to cultivate

_____
_____
_____
_____
_____
_____
_____
_____
_____
_____
_____
_____
_____
_____
_____
_____
_____
_____
_____
_____
_____
_____
_____
_____
_____

Template 9: List of
Daily Good Habits to cultivate

_____

_____

_____

_____

_____

_____

_____

_____

_____

_____

_____

_____

_____

_____

_____

_____

_____

_____

_____

_____

_____

_____

_____

_____

_____

Template 10:
Individual Good Habit Daily Progress

Good Habit that I want to do more often:

_____

Date:	How many times per day:

Template 10:
Individual Good Habit Daily Progress

Good Habit that I want to do more often:

_____

_____

Date:	How many times per day:

CONCLUSION

You can change your habits. And you don't have to be a psychology professor to do it either. In this book, we shared some little-known ways you can start changing your own behavior today, without the help of an expensive therapist or coach. Breaking old habits and creating new ones can be easier than you think. Remember, it takes around 21 days to form a new habit, but if you are breaking an old habit or replacing the old habit with a new one, it will take a bit longer, around 2-3 months.

It is possible to change your habits and create the life that you've always wanted! All you need is some determination, a written or visual plan and a couple of months of hard work. You can create the YOU that you've always known you could be. Just take it one step at a time, be patient, and believe in yourself. I know you can do it!

INDEX

Printed in Great Britain
by Amazon